A PORTRAIT OF

PORTSMOUTH
GOSPORT AND SOUTHSEA

HOME OF THE ROYAL NAVY

A PORTRAIT OF

PORTSMOUTH

GOSPORT AND SOUTHSEA

HOME OF THE ROYAL NAVY

IAIN McGOWAN

HALSGROVE

First published in Great Britain in 2005

Image copyright © 2005 Iain McGowan
unless otherwise stated
Text copyright © 2005 Iain McGowan

British Library Cataloguing-in-Publication Data
A CIP record for this title is available from the British Library

ISBN 1 84114 454 1

HALSGROVE
Halsgrove House
Lower Moor Way
Tiverton, Devon EX16 6SS
Tel: 01884 243242
Fax: 01884 243325
email: sales@halsgrove.com
website: www.halsgrove.com

Printed and bound by D'Auria Industrie Grafiche Spa, Italy

CONTENTS

MAPS OF THE AREA COVERED BY THIS BOOK

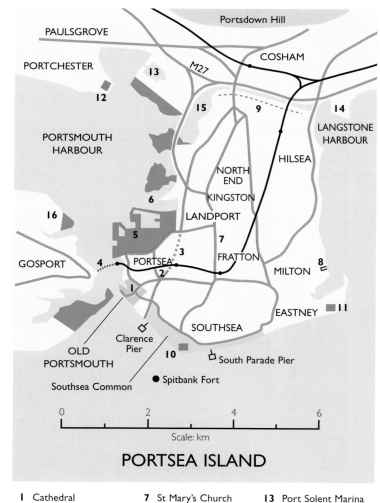

PAULSGROVE

Portsdown Hill

PORTCHESTER

COSHAM

M27

13

12

15

9

14

LANGSTONE
HARBOUR

PORTSMOUTH
HARBOUR

HILSEA

NORTH
END

KINGSTON

6

LANDPORT

16

5

7

3

GOSPORT

4

PORTSEA

FRATTON

2

MILTON

8

EASTNEY

11

SOUTHSEA

Clarence
Pier

OLD
PORTSMOUTH

10

South Parade Pier

Southsea Common

Spitbank Fort

0   2   4   6

Scale: km

PORTSEA ISLAND

1 Cathedral	7 St Mary's Church	13 Port Solent Marina
2 The Guildhall	8 Milton Lock	14 Farlington Marshes
3 Commercial Road	9 Hilsea Lines	15 Ports Creek
4 Gosport Ferry	10 Southsea Castle	16 Priddy's Hard
5 RN Dockyard	11 Fort Cumberland	
6 Ferry Port	12 Portchester Castle	

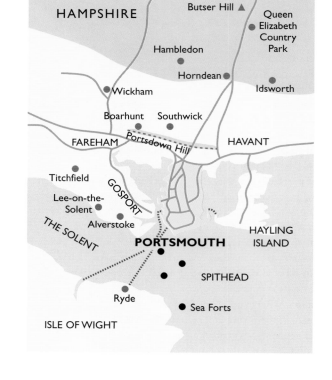

HAMPSHIRE

Butser Hill ▲

Queen
Elizabeth
Country
Park

Hambledon

Horndean

Idsworth

Wickham

Boarhunt

Southwick

FAREHAM

Portsdown Hill

HAVANT

Titchfield

GOSPORT

Lee-on-the-
Solent

Alverstoke

HAYLING
ISLAND

THE SOLENT

PORTSMOUTH

SPITHEAD

Ryde

Sea Forts

ISLE OF WIGHT

	Portsea Island
	RN Establishments
	South Downs
————	Railways
————	Major Roads
··········	Ferries

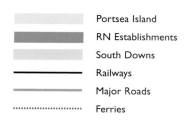

N
W   E
S

INTRODUCTION

Portsmouth's unique island site, surrounded on three sides by sheltered waters and protected from the north by mainland Portsdown Hill, has ensured the city's place in English History. In a sense its natural topography has been Portsmouth's greatest architect and planner. The story of Portsmouth is the story of the country's association with the sea, trade, Empire and above all, defence and the Royal Navy. For over 2000 years Portsmouth has seen departures of naval fleets and military personnel to wars in every part of the globe, its street and pub names acting as mute reminders and a celebration of past glories; its parks and waterfront still filled with carved stone memorials engraved with the names of those who never returned.

The arrival of the Romans in the first century AD marked the beginning of major human occupation of the Portsmouth region. The potential safety of Portsmouth Harbour provided an ideal site for a fleet anchorage and defensive fortifications, the latter culminating in the construction of Portchester Castle some 200 years later. Following the Norman invasion a small settlement began to grow on neighbouring Portsea Island at the harbour's entrance. It was formally founded as a town (Portesmue) by the Norman landowner, Jean de Gisors in 1180. The chancel and transepts of the town's first church are now incorporated into the present-day cathedral and the town's layout is still reflected in the street plan of Old Portsmouth.

In the twelfth and thirteenth centuries both King Richard I and King John realised the strategic advantage of the site as a reliable port enabling assembly and embarkation of armies to France and the south. It was during this period that the first docks were built. The destructive French raids during the fourteenth century only served to emphasise the town's growing importance and the requirement for some form of systematic defence. Initial construction of earthworks and a moat around the town were soon upgraded to stone fortifications and by the end of the fifteenth century Portsmouth, together with Gosport across the harbour mouth, was one of the most protected areas in Northern Europe.

The building of the country's first dry dock during the same period marked the beginning of an industrialised dockyard confirmed by King Henry VII's declaration of Portsmouth as a Royal Dockyard and garrison town. From Henry VIII's reign, with its antagonistic attitude towards the French, up until the later years of the nineteenth century, Portsmouth's growth was entirely dependent upon the dockyard's development and a succession of European wars. Its local economy was totally reliant on decisions made in the high offices of the Foreign Office and the Admiralty.

By 1700 increasingly sophisticated warships were starting to be built within the yard and with this the need for greater repair and servicing facilities. The term 'Royal Navy' was in general use and the harbour recognised as the chief naval base in the country. Ramparts and fortifications of the most advanced design surrounded the town and Daniel Defoe writing in the 1720s on his second journey through Britain arrived in Portsmouth to:-

the largest fortification, beyond comparison, that we have in England. The situation of this place is such, that it is chosen for the best security to the Navy above all places in Britain; the entrance into the harbour is safe, but very narrow, guarded on both sides by terrible platforms of cannon particularly on the point.

He had reached a town that seemed to have its own unique vocabulary based on the descriptions of defensive features. The terms banquette, bastion, berm, caponier, casemate, counterscarp, embrasure, enciente, en decharge, enfilade, glacis, merlons, ravelin, redan, salient and terre-plein were almost part of a different world and in many respects Portsmouth's situation was just that.

Throughout the eighteenth century the Royal Navy steadily grew in size and influence to become the largest single employer in Britain. By the Napoleonic Wars the dockyard was at the leading edge of the industrial revolution and described as the 'world's greatest industrial complex'. Outside of its walls the new town of Portsea was expanding to cater for the increasingly large workforce unable to find room within the confines of the old town. The massive extensions to the yard in the middle of the nineteenth century and the arrival of the railway in 1847 accelerated the demand for more housing and during this century alone the population grew almost six-fold to 190,000 by 1901. A drift by the more wealthy professional and officer families to the new speculative suburb-cum-resort of Southsea had started and the once rural areas of Kingston, Landport and Milton were also fast becoming new towns in their own right. From the 1860s the entire area, including the Gosport peninsular, was being surrounded by the massive Palmerstonian fortifications, strengthening the existing defences because of uncertainty over Napoleon III's military ambitions and making Portsmouth the most heavily defended place in the world.

By the First World War the dockyard had reached its zenith, employing some 26,000 workers and the town borough had not only engulfed most of Portsea Island but was starting to spread out on to mainland Hampshire with Cosham, Farlington, Paulsgrove and Portchester being slowly taken over and built upon. 1927 was marked by Portsmouth's creation as a new diocese with its church of St Thomas of Canterbury becoming its new cathedral. Work to extend the building started shortly after but due to the interruption of the Second World War, was not finally completed until 1991.

During the Second World War the new city suffered terribly from bombing, the naval base and dockyard making it a prime target. In 67 air raids large areas were laid waste, many lives lost and over 65,000 properties destroyed or damaged to varying degrees. In addition to nearly 10,000 Portsmouth based sailors lost in the First World War, almost 15,000 sailors and marines were killed in the second conflict. Over the immediate years that followed, large numbers of the displaced population were re-housed on the mainland in new estates, most notably Leigh Park in the borough of Havant. On Portsea Island rebuilding slowly started to take place resulting in the many controversial and sometimes bland medium and high rise structures still to be seen today. Only later were funds diverted to improving existing housing stock. With a combination of the city's defining townscape of terraced housing laid out in a grid-iron fashion and its 1960's inner city blocks, Portsmouth is now one of the most densely populated urban areas in Europe with all the attendant problems that the late twentieth century has produced.

As Britain has gradually lost its Empire, its Navy too has been scaled down together with the dockyard. A large surface fleet is no longer thought necessary, the days of building warships within the yard have finished and many of the facilities from the past have become redundant. However, not all of the Navy's famous names have disappeared. Many have been used or transferred to the numerous shore-based establishments still surviving in various quarters of the City. HMS *Centurian*, *Collingwood*, *Dolphin*, *Dryad*, *Excellent*, *Nelson*, *Sultan*, *St Vincent*, to name just a few, are an essential part of the training of today's modern Navy.

The past is also becoming valued for its heritage interest and in some cases its suitability for conversion to more modern requirements. Museums have sprung up around the city, often in refurbished naval or military buildings. Luxury apartments have been engineered from redundant store or warehousing and Old Portsmouth in particular has become a fashionable place to live with its new developments around the Camber and waterfront. The 'historic dockyard' itself with its showpieces HMS *Victory* and HMS *Warrior*, along with the remains of the *Mary Rose*, the Royal Naval museum and the new 'Action Stations' has become a leading national tourist attraction. As the twenty-first century dawned the city received a new stimulus in the shape of the multi-million pound Renaissance of Portsmouth Harbour Project supported by the Millennium Commission. Incorporating the Millennium Promenade 2000 'chain motif' walkway, linking many places of interest along its harbour-side route and with the associated redevelopment of Gunwharf Quays together with other newly landscaped historic areas, Portsmouth Harbour is starting to become quite literally a world heritage site. Above it all the 170m high Spinnaker Tower, the new national landmark at the harbour entrance and centrepiece of the entire project, is nearing completion and will soon undoubtedly draw many further visitors to the city.

There may not be so many arrivals and departures of grey painted warships these days threading their way through the harbour's narrow entrance past Henry VII's Round Tower, but the luxury ferries from France and Spain are arriving in ever increasing numbers. Portsmouth's Continental Ferry Port is now one of the busiest in the country; the thirteen-year-old University has become a major factor in the local economy and, with the arrival of several large foreign business companies into the area together with an explosion of new technological industries, the prospects of this unique island city look bright. 'Pompey' is still a strange mixture of the old and the new, sometimes attractive, sometimes down at heel, but always of interest. There is a deeply rooted pride that comes from such a vigorous and historic past. This year, 2005 – the year of the sea, marks the 200th anniversary of the Battle of Trafalgar, an event to be celebrated in style. This book is also a celebration, of the heritage and future of a great English city, home of the Royal Navy.

Photographic Notes

From the outset it was decided to incorporate aspects of both Gosport and Southsea into this book as well as the general surrounding area. Portsea Island alone would not describe the City of Portsmouth. When considering what lies on the mainland around the city, one can argue that the associated towns of Fareham and Havant should also be included but regrettably due to the limitations of space this has not been found possible. The truth of the matter is that there are simply too many interesting aspects of Portsmouth to insert into one book! It should also be noted that most places featured within the book are accessible to the general public and are not situated within restricted naval controlled areas.

Pentax LX 35mm cameras supported by a series of prime lenses of different focal lengths were used for all images. Film stock was either Kodachrome 64 or Fuji Velvia.

The view looking southwest over the quiet inner reaches of Portsmouth Harbour from near Wicor Hard. It was the natural haven of the harbour containing some 40 square kilometres of sheltered and often deep water that was the initial reason for the founding of Portsmouth and which has continued to be of such value to the present day. This coupled with the spacious anchorage at Spithead, shielded by the Isle of Wight, meant that Portsmouth's natural geography shaped its future.

Part of the 1km-long defensive Roman wall to Portchester Castle with the city approaches in the background. The walling is over 3m thick and 6m high with a series of projecting bastions for use with catapult artillery. These walls have been described as some of the finest preserved Roman walls in northern Europe.

Early Days
PORTCHESTER
and
OLD PORTSMOUTH

Portchester Castle is a spectacular feature of the harbour. It was built by the Romans in the third century AD as one of the 'Saxon Shore' forts – a coastal defence system stretching from Portsmouth to the Wash. Occupying an area of almost 4 hectares and surrounded on three sides by water, the castle dominates any approach from the sea to the landward areas. It is evidence of the first major human occupation of the Portsmouth region and marks the beginning of the harbour's importance in naval heritage.

During the reign of Henry I, following the Norman invasion, it was transformed into a grand royal castle by the addition of its massive keep and inner bailey. Its uses in the following centuries, between periods of neglect, ranged from a residence for Richard II to a prison during the Napoleonic Wars. Today it is in the care of English Heritage. *Left:* Looking down from the keep on to the ruins of Richard II's medieval palace within the castle walls.

Above left: Evidence of the castle's grim years as a prison can be found in the numerous examples of French grafitti carved in the stonework. At one time over 9000 prisoners were held here.

Above right: The castle keep as shown on the name plaque of Castle House in the adjacent village street. The old village centre of Portchester is still a delightful collection of mostly eighteenth century houses. Considering the urban sprawl of modern Portchester spread out below Portsdown Hill, it is astonishing that the compact, older area along Castle Street has remained unspoilt for so long.

Right: Within the walls is the ancient Augustinian priory church of St Mary founded by Henry I in 1133. It is believed that a Roman temple originally stood on the same site followed by a timber Saxon church. Part of the Norman arch above the west door is shown here. Signs of the zodiac above the capitals celebrated the changing of the seasons in medieval times.

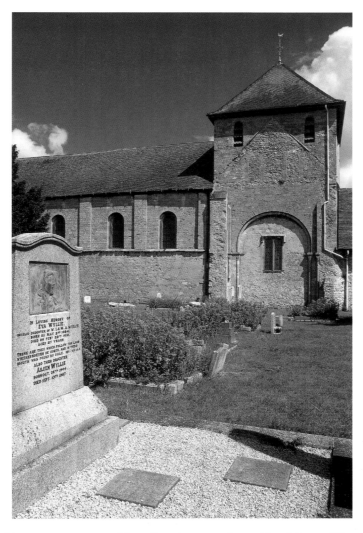

After the Norman canons moved from Portchester in the middle of the twelfth century, the church was allowed to fall into disrepair for some 400 years before restoration during the reign of Elizabeth I, by which time the south transept had already been demolished. This view of the church clearly shows where the south transept once joined the building and the subsequent infilling. In the foreground is the family grave of the well-known Portsmouth marine artist W. L. Wyllie, his wife Marion and daughters Eva and Aileen. St Mary's now acts as the parish church of Portchester.

The entrance to Portsmouth harbour with Old Portsmouth and its spit to the right and Gosport 'over the water' to the left on the western shore. The width of the channel is extremely narrow, being only 230m at one point. Due to the harbour's early importance as a sheltered anchorage and assembly area for fleets, a small settlement slowly formed at its entrance, being officially founded as a town (Portesmue) in 1180 by the Norman wool merchant and landowner Jean de Gisors. This was to become the area we now know as Old Portsmouth.

Tower House in the immediate foreground was the home of the artist W. L. Wyllie whilst in the harbour itself the 'fast cat' catamaran ferry from the Isle of Wight is just arriving. The naval dockyard is in the middle distance and beyond are the slopes of Portsdown Hill. Flood defence works are being carried out at the water's edge of what is now one of the busiest waterways in Europe.

Fishing boats at anchor at Camber Quay. Once the town's original port, being developed by the Normans in the twelfth century, this working quay still houses a thriving fish market. In the past it handled all types of trade, coal remaining active until well into the twentieth century.

Becoming increasingly surrounded by modern housing, flats and apartments, the quay is also included within the route of the Millennium Promenade 2000 'chain motif' walkway linking many places of interest along its route around both east and west shores of the harbour. At one time a bridge spanned the waterway, dividing the Camber into inner and outer areas, but this was removed to give more wharfage accommodation. The Isle of Wight car ferry services to Fishbourne depart from nearby.

The tower of the Cathedral Church of St Thomas of Canterbury rising above some of the new apartments seen from across Camber Quay. Set in the heart of historic Old Portsmouth, the cathedral has had a long and interesting history. It was initially built as a simple chapel in about 1185 to serve the slowly growing town on land given by Jean de Gisors and dedicated to Thomas Beckett, the murdered Archbishop of Canterbury. From this original building only the chancel and transepts now remain. In the fourteenth century it became a parish church and was also used as a lighthouse and lookout post in both times of peace and war. As a result of the latter usage the building was badly damaged during the Civil War and it was not until the reign of Charles II that rebuilding, including a new tower and nave, was completed. The wooden cupola, with a lantern for shipping on top, was added to the tower in 1703. In this condition the building remained the parish church until 1927.

In 1927 the new Diocese of Portsmouth was created and the church chosen as the cathedral for the new bishop and people of the city. By 1930 work had begun to enlarge the building for its new role based on the designs of Sir Charles Nicholson. However all construction ceased at the outbreak of the Second World War. Attempts to finish the structure in the 1960s proved unsuccessful and it was not until 1991 that the Cathedral as we know it today was finally completed, by then under the appointment of the architect Michael Drury.

The photograph shows part of the original south transept on the right, the rebuilt tower with its wooden cupola and the later outer walls of the quire and nave built between 1935 and 1939.

The striking and unusual west doorway, dedicated by the bishop in 1997. Designed by Bryan Kneale, the doors were made at the Sculpture Factory under the direction of John Crisfield.

In memory of ADMIRAL
SIR BERTRAM RAMSAY
killed in action 1945 who
commanded the seaborne
forces at Dunkirk 1940

and Normandy 1944
here are remembered
also those under his
command who were killed
during these operations

The two lower lights of the D-Day window in the Holy Martyrs' chapel. The window was a gift from the D-Day and Normandy Fellowship in 1984 – the fortieth anniversary of the D-Day and Normandy landings. The panels depict the two most famous seaborne actions of the Second World War; the rescue of British troops at the evacuation of Dunkirk in 1940 and the landing of allied forces on D-Day, 6 June 1944. They are a memorial to Admiral Sir Bertram Ramsay who commanded the seaborne forces in both actions.

The slate gravestone that covers the bones of a crew member of Henry VIII's flagship *Mary Rose* which foundered in the Solent in 1545. These remains were discovered when the ship was brought to the surface again in 1982 prior to restoration in Portsmouth. The stone is the work of John Skelton and the grave is situated in the Navy Aisle, just one of the many indicators of the cathedral's close connections with the seafaring community and the Royal Navy.

A view taken inside the new nave and looking towards the seventeenth-century tower arch and baptistry. The quire and original twelfth-century chancel are beyond.

Over the eighteen centuries since the construction of Portchester Castle, the harbour has seen a constant succession of departures and arrivals of fighting ships to and from all parts of the globe. Here friends and relatives on top of the Round Tower at the harbour entrance welcome the return of D87 HMS *Newcastle* back to Portsmouth after a tour of duty. The Round Tower completed in 1422 and later much modified, was the first of the harbour mouth's stone fortifications, built as a result of a revival of hostilities with France. Between this and a wooden tower on the Gosport side a 'mighty chain of iron' was laid across the harbour mouth that could be raised by capstans and floats to prevent enemy vessels from entering the harbour. The Gosport tower was later superseded by Fort Blockhouse ie a building designed to block an enemy attack.

Crowds line the beach at the harbour entrance to watch the departure of the aircraft carrier HMS *Ark Royal* sailing for the Gulf War in early 2003. The low winter sunshine shows up part of the fortifications of Point Battery on the extreme right. These were built under the supervision of Charles II's chief engineer Sir Bernard de Gomme in the 1600s and later reconstructed to strengthen the Round Tower defences.

A quieter scene on the same beach. The beach below Point Battery is a favourite location for fishermen and sunbathers enjoying the afternoon sunshine as its warmth is reflected back from the stonework. The area is known as the 'Hot Walls'.

The first defensive earthworks and moat to enclose Old Portsmouth were constructed in the fourteenth century following the recognition of defence requirements and the appointment of a military governor. A few years later these were upgraded to stone starting with the Round Tower. Sir Bernard de Gomme was instructed to totally reconstruct the Portsmouth defences increasing the size of ramparts and bastions, adding larger batteries and introducing a series of fortified ravelins in the moat. Work on a smaller scale was also carried out at Gosport. In their turn many of these new defences were upgraded over the centuries.

Looking south along the walkway above Point Battery. The Square Tower is on the left and the Isle of Wight coast in the distance on the right across the waters of Spithead.

The Square Tower was another of Henry VIII's additions to the town's fortifications and completed in 1494. It was later used as a powder magazine until the construction of a new magazine at Priddy's Hard on the Gosport shore, away from the crowded confines of Old Portsmouth.

By the middle of the nineteenth century with new developments in military technology it was realised that the enclosing walls and many of the defences were fast becoming obsolete. Today most have been removed or in-filled except for those flanking the harbour entrance. Here the Round and Square Towers, parts of Point Battery, the Saluting Platform and Long Curtain now form yet another part of the Millennium Promenade 2000 walkway, allowing all to enjoy the constantly changing maritime scene.

A view across the recently landscaped area of Grand Parade. The town's main guardhouse, erected during the reign of George III near the adjacent Platform Battery, was situated on the parade to the left of this scene. It housed both drunken soldiers, soldiers who had broken leave and those poor unfortunates picked up by the naval press gangs. The sentries manning the town's gates and walls were also posted from here. The guardhouse was demolished in 1883.

The part ruined Royal Garrison Church. Located near Grand Parade (and its adjacent ramparts), the church was originally part of the Domus Dei (God's House) or the Hospital of St John and St Nicholas. Founded in 1212 as a hospice it sheltered pilgrims from overseas bound for the holy shrines of Canterbury, Chichester and Winchester. During the Dissolution of the 1500s all the hospice buildings were closed, being converted firstly into military stores and then later to a residence for the Governor of Portsmouth. By 1826 most had been demolished except for what is now the Garrison Church. Thoroughly restored in the 1860s, the church continued to be used until the Second World War when a firebomb raid on the city in 1941 left the nave as a roofless shell with only the original fine Early English chancel still intact.

Today this remaining portion of the church, once known as the Cathedral Church of the British Army, is open to the public and a small number of services, mainly by local Ex-Service Associations, are still held there.

A portion of one of the windows situated in the south wall of the Royal Garrison Church illustrating the church being set alight during the fire bomb raid, the Solent forts and searchlights below and silhouettes of planes flying in formation overhead.

Within the remaining building are many mementoes and displays of its interesting history including the marriage of Charles II, visits by James II and George III, visits by allied sovereigns during the nineteenth century and the city's military past.

Left: The Landport Gate in St George's Road. At one time the principal entrance to Old Portsmouth when still fortified and enclosed, this is the only town gate to survive in its original position. It was built around 1760 and once flanked by ramparts with a moat in front. The town's walls also included King William's Gate, the Quay Gate and King James' Gate. A contemporary account describes, 'These gates and roads are so completely overlooked by lines of fortifications that the out-goers and in-comers are wholly at the mercy of those who govern the ramparts'.

Right: This plaque to Admiral Lord Nelson was formerly sited over the Penny Street entrance to the George Hotel destroyed by bombing in 1941. It records Nelson's final departure from Portsmouth, probably via King William's Gate, to board HMS *Victory* prior to his death at the Battle of Trafalgar.

Looking back along the newly landscaped area of the Saluting Platform towards the Square Tower and harbour mouth with a Brittany Ferries ship entering the harbour. Together with the Square Tower, the platform was another of the Tudor defences initially designed to carry cannon. With the adjacent Spur Redoubt, Long Curtain and Point batteries a continuous line of defensive positions faced the harbour approach for several hundred metres. A semaphore station was added to the roof of the Square Tower around 1823 only to be moved to a new site above the Sail Loft and Rigging House in the dockyard a few years later. The semaphore superseded a shutter telegraph system inaugurated in the late eighteenth century by which messages could be sent to Portsmouth along a line of hill-top stations from the Admiralty. The Square Tower is now used for private and civil functions.

The colourful mural to be found on the side of the Bridge Tavern close to Camber Quay is based on Thomas Rowlandson's watercolour of Portsmouth Point and vividly conveys in caricature the atmosphere of local life in days gone by. Point, at the northern extremity of the spit at Old Portsmouth, but outside the town's walls, was notorious for its numerous pubs and alehouses and was the haunt of fishermen, sailors, smugglers and ladies of ill repute. It was also regarded as the main meeting ground of the infamous press gangs that forcibly enlisted young men to join the Navy. The area's colourful past, its associations with exotic cargoes and its once insanitary conditions earned it the name of Spice Island.

The classic view from Point overlooking the harbour, the re-developed Gunwharf Quays and the rising Spinnaker Tower. Now landscaped as part of the Renaissance of Portsmouth Harbour 2000 and including a further section of the 'chain motif' walkway, Point is an ideal vantage area to view the maritime events within the harbour. William Walton in his overture *Portsmouth Point* immortalised the scene in music.

Old Portsmouth, looking along Lombard Street. Despite the savage bombing during the Second World War, many of the earlier houses in Old Portsmouth have remained and this attractive row in Lombard Street includes some of the finest. Most of the houses in the old town were re-built or re-faced during the Georgian period leaving an inner timber framework, possibly dating back to the late sixteenth century, intact. Locally characteristic shallow bow or canted bay windows were often used and many façades stuccoed and simplified.

Looking northwards up West Street towards Point and the harbour. The Spice Island Inn is at the end on the right, opposite the Still and West public house – both highly popular venues for residents and visitors enjoying the harbour views. By the mid nineteenth century Old Portsmouth had become somewhat isolated, Portsea and Landport had grown enormously and Southsea was emerging as a fashionable resort. The old town found itself cut off by its geographical nature and general progress. Before the Second World War it was described as decayed and picturesque and what survived the bombing raids has now been discreetly restored into an increasingly desirable quarter, in-filled with modern up-market flats and apartments.

This page and opposite: Scenes and details around Old Portsmouth.

Note the Dutch gables to Nos 1 – 3 Lombard Street *(top right)*. Broad Street *(top left)* is the principal thoroughfare leading down the spit to Point which at one time was separated from the rest of the old town by King James' Gate. It ensured respectable townsfolk were kept apart from the disrepute of Point! The Sallyport Tearooms *(middle left)* are named after the nearby Sally Port – an opening cut through the defensive walls of Point Battery for access purposes to make a 'sally' or sortie.

Top middle: This house in Broad Street features a painting of HMS *Fortitude* between two of its upper floor windows. The plaque outside Buckingham House in the High Street *(bottom right)* refers to the assassination of the Duke of Buckingham in 1628 whilst the white painted weatherboarded Quebec House *(bottom left)* at the harbour's edge was originally built as a salt water bathing house about 1754.

The main entrance to Portsmouth Grammar School. Portsmouth's oldest school, now one of the country's leading independent day schools, was founded by Dr William Smith in 1732. Originally sited in Penny Street, it has occupied the former Cambridge Barracks off the High Street since 1926. Fully co-educational after 1991, pupils from the ages of four to eighteen years are taught to the highest levels of academic achievement. The school prides itself by placing considerable emphasis on public service and extra curricular activities and has an outstanding cadet force. It is also heavily involved with the newly formed Portsmouth Arts Festival.

John Pounds' memorial stone and replica workshop at the side of the Memorial Church Unitarian in the High Street. John Pounds was born in 1766 in what is now Highbury Street and initially became a dockyard apprentice. Forced to find other work after an accident left him crippled, he became a cobbler. A good friend to the poor of the neighbourhood he eventually established a school for neglected children in his cobbler's shop and for thirty years he fed, taught and clothed hundreds of poor children.

He died on New Year's Day 1839 and the stone marks his grave, but his fame had spread and the Ragged School movement had started to establish a number of similar schools, John being acknowledged as their originator.

HMS *Victory*. Referred to as the most famous ship in British Naval History and the oldest commissioned warship in the world, HMS *Victory* has been berthed at No 2 Dry Dock within the dockyard since 1922 and has for many years been the very symbol of Portsmouth and its naval heritage. Her building commenced at Chatham in 1759 taking six years and consuming an estimated 40 hectares of oak woodland. Displacing 3500 tons and with a crew of 850 and 104 guns, she was a 'first rate' warship and the sixth of the Royal Navy to bear the name *Victory*. Between 1778 and 1797 she saw considerable active service in many parts of the globe including Ushant, Gibraltar, Toulon, Corsica and Cape St Vincent. It was at this latter engagement against the Spanish that the names of the *Victory* and the then Commodore Horatio Nelson became synonymous.

Formative Years
PORTSEA
and
THE NAVAL DOCKYARD

After a major refit (the 'great repair') between 1801 and 1803 and a further two year's service in the Mediterranean, HMS *Victory* was sent as flagship of Admiral Lord Nelson in September 1805 to take over command of the British Fleet blockading Cadiz. It was this operation that culminated in the destruction of the combined French and Spanish fleets off Cape Trafalgar on 21 October 1805 in what has been described as one of the most decisive naval battles ever fought and the sad death of Nelson himself. Severely damaged HMS *Victory* returned to Portsmouth in December 1805; Nelson's body being interred in St Paul's Cathedral a month later as a national hero.

With Portsmouth Harbour being used as an anchorage for naval fleets from at least Roman times, it was inevitable that there would be a need for boat building and maintenance facilities. The first distinctive docks were built in the twelfth and thirteenth centuries at the command of King Richard I and King John, to be followed by the first dry dock in the late fifteenth century. With the establishment of a permanent navy during the reign of Henry VIII followed by a re-direction of resources to the south coast by William III in 1690, the dockyard began to grow at an increasing rate over the succeeding centuries. Waterside land and areas of the harbour were reclaimed, new docks built together with workshop and stores facilities and by 1817 the yard was noted as 'the largest naval arsenal in the world'. The role of the dockyard was to construct, repair and maintain ships and with the increase in numbers and size of naval vessels, the 'great' extension of the dockyard in the 1860s, almost trebling its size, enabled the very largest of warships to be built and serviced. By the twentieth century the dockyard occupied an area of almost 150 hectares and at its zenith employed a workforce of some 26,000.

Following extensive repairs completed in 1808 and further tours of duty, HMS *Victory* finally became flagship of the Portsmouth Command in 1824, her fighting days over. After almost 100 years afloat in the harbour and grave concern about the state of her timbers, she was placed in No 2 Dry Dock in 1922. A public appeal was launched by the Society of Nautical Research to raise money for her restoration to the appearance she bore at Trafalgar. With the success of this appeal, restoration was completed in 1928 and the ship opened for public viewing

Above: A scene along one of the vessel's three gun decks. About 500 crew lived on these decks which were often dark, smelly and damp as the gun ports were generally kept closed unless in battle situations. Hammocks were slung from the timbers between the guns. Note the cannon balls stored on the left.

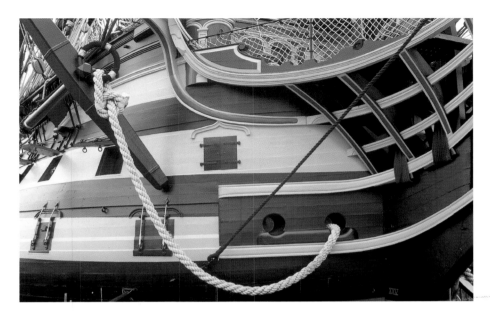

Details of HMS *Victory*. The hull is of English oak, with outer and inner skins, and over 60cm thick. The overall length of the ship is 69m and her main mast rises to a height of almost 63m above the dockside. The figurehead at the bows dates from the refit of 1801-03 and comprises two cupids supporting an oval shield with the Royal Arms emblazoned and the Royal Crown above. Below is the motto 'Dieu et mon droit'.

The naval dockyard is one of the best examples of Georgian industrial premises in the country, containing many fine brick buildings dating back to the eighteenth century and built with a solid functional elegance. Its later Victorian structures featured architecture on a monumental scale and appearance with considerable use of iron in their construction. At the present time most of the yard is restricted to service personnel except on special occasions, access for visitors being confined to the route between the main gate and HMS *Victory*. However, within these constraints a general impression can be formed of the nature and scale of the dockyard and its fascinating history. *Below left:* A tablet records the building of the original dockyard wall in 1711 some of which is still standing. *Above:* The timber No 7 boathouse of 1875 and yellow brick No 6 boathouse of 1843, originally constructed as mast houses, sited around the mast pond which is now used for small boat exhibits. *Left:* No 10 store of 1778 with its new clock tower and cupola replacing that destroyed in the bombing.

A portion of the east window of the dockyard church of St Ann reveals a stylised birds-eye view of part of the dockyard as seen from the semaphore tower in 1945 after the ending of the Second World War. The window by Hugh Easton is a memorial to all those who worked in and sailed from Portsmouth and who lost their lives in the war. The church of St Ann situated within the dockyard walls was opened in 1786 replacing an earlier chapel built to answer the needs of dockyard residents and employees. The plain classical brick building – the parish church of the naval base – has been beautifully restored although shortened by 5m due to war damage. With its graceful proportions it has been described as one of the city's most attractive churches. It contains many items of historic naval interest including a granite font carved by convicts, a display case from the HMS *Hood* Association, battle ensigns, a silver plated lectern, a magnificent central chandelier and ceiling rose, candlesticks presented as a memorial to those lost in the sinking of HMS *Royal Oak* at Scapa Flow, an historic silver display, a carved coat of arms originally mounted on the dockyard commissioner's barge in the early 1700s and numerous plaques, tablets and memorials around the walls to individuals and ships' companies.

An almost timeless scene as HMS *Warrior* (the 'Black Snake') looms out of the mist on a damp winter's morning. HMS *Warrior* was the largest and most powerful warship of her age when she was commissioned in 1861. She was the first ocean-going, iron-hulled battleship and with her armour plating, steam engine and heavy armament, she was more than a match for any other warship afloat. Built as an answer to Napoleon III's growing fleet, Napoleon was forced to rein-in his military ambitions despite *Warrior* never being challenged in battle.

Only fourteen years later *Warrior* was obsolete, such was the speed in the advance of naval design. However, due to her immense structural strength she survived until 1979 in a series of roles ranging from a stationary depot ship, a torpedo school ship and finally a fuel pontoon hulk in Pembrokeshire. In that year she was taken over by the Maritime Trust and towed to Hartlepool where, under the inspiration of John Smith, she was completely restored to original condition working from meticulous details laid down by a fourteen-year-old midshipman in 1861. She left Hartlepool and arrived in Portsmouth under tow in June 1987. She was docked at a purpose-built berth to become another priceless asset to the city's naval heritage area.

No 1 Dry Dock with Monitor M33 undergoing restoration work. Behind is the aircraft carrier HMS *Invincible*. M33 is one of only two British First World War ships to have survived the wars and ravages of time. Built as a monitor or coastal bombardment vessel in 1915, she was one of five similar vessels each armed with two 150mm guns. Originally seeing action in the Dardanelles campaign and the Russian Civil War, she was later put to various uses. In 1987 she was purchased by the Hartlepool Ship Preservation Trust followed by Hampshire County Council who, in 1991, berthed her in the dockyard, starting restoration work four years later. No 1 Dry Dock completed in 1801 of stone construction was rebuilt from the original timber South Dock of 1703.

The remains of the Tudor warship the *Mary Rose* undergoing preservation treatment in the Mary Rose Ship Hall. The *Mary Rose* was completed in 1511, built under the orders of Henry VIII for use as his flagship. She was one of the earliest warships to carry heavy guns, these being placed nearer the waterline than in earlier practice in order to keep the vessel stable. In 1545 during a skirmish with the French in the Solent, and watched by the King from Southsea Castle, the *Mary Rose* capsized and sank with a crew of some 700 men. It is thought that this was due to the gun ports being kept open in rough seas. Slowly over the centuries much of the vessel and her contents were buried in the seabed and despite early salvage attempts, it was not until 1978 that excavation and recovery of some 19,000 artefacts began, culminating in the vessel herself being raised in 1982 by the Mary Rose Trust under the direction of Margaret Rule. Watched on television by an estimated 60 million people around the world, she was towed into the dockyard on a purpose built cradle and placed in No 3 Dry Dock over which a temporary hall had been built to allow recording and conservation work to start. Since 1994 the ship has been sprayed with a water-soluble wax which penetrates her timbers. This process will take at least fifteen years to complete and should preserve this unique vessel for all time.

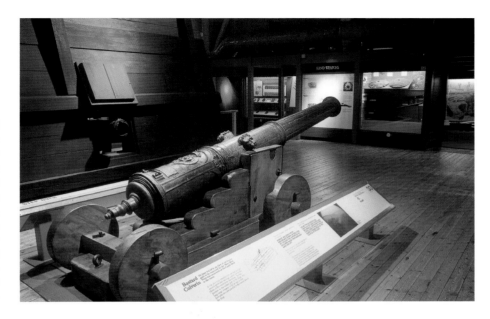

A few of the many thousands of objects discovered during the recovery of the *Mary Rose* and now displayed within the Mary Rose Museum. The sheer variety of items paints a remarkable picture of life in Tudor times. There are not only the more obvious finds of the ship's main guns, each individually cast in bronze to a different design and with their associated shot, but also unique collections of longbows and arrows, pewter, items of clothing, personal possessions, medicines, seeds, remains of insects, dice, coins, pens, ink pots, cooking artefacts, sundials and many, many more. It was their burial within the soft Solent silt that ensured the preservation of so many fascinating items.

Several boat companies operate trips around Portsmouth Harbour especially in the summer months. Generally these last about an hour and take in the harbour mouth fortifications, Gunwharf Quays, HMS *Warrior*, parts of the Naval Dockyard, the Ferry Port, Gosport and Haslar Marina. On a fine day it is an excellent way to see these locations. *Above:* Passengers looking at some of the vessels moored in the Continental Ferry Port. The Ferry Port itself is now one of the busiest ports in Britain with considerable freight traffic, luxury cruise ferries and fast catamarans travelling to the Channel Islands and at least six continental destinations.

A misty early morning view of the dockyard seen from a departing continental ferry with the aircraft carrier HMS *Ark Royal* at anchor. One of the delights of travelling to and from Portsmouth by ferry is the series of superb views one can obtain of the dockyard and spotting which warships are at 'home'.

With the growth of the dockyard in the eighteenth century requiring an increasingly large workforce and due to the walled constraints of Old Portsmouth, the new town of Portsea (between the old town and the dockyard) began to grow and in a relatively short period its population had outstripped that of Old Portsmouth. At the same time there was a religious revival in England and these two factors encouraged a wave of new church building in Portsea. St George's church was paid for and built by the people themselves in 1753 using 15 shipwrights from the dockyard plus 'three gentlemen, one carpenter, one tallow chandler and one grocer'. Constructed in brick in an American Colonial style, it was the first Anglican church to serve the new town. Badly damaged during the Second World War it is only recently that major restoration work has been completed and the church assigned a conventional district. Rodney Hubbock in his *Portsea Island Churches* described St George's as a model of everything a city church should be.

Historical aspects of Portsea. *Bottom right:* Housing in Curzon Howe Road. These were the first council houses in Portsmouth built in 1910 to replace cleared slum dwellings. *Bottom left:* The entrance gateway to the shore based HMS *Nelson*, the Royal Naval Barracks originally built in the early twentieth century and now much modernised. *Top:* A reminder of the period prior to the 1870 Education Act when elementary education became available for all. Up to this time children from poorer backgrounds had to rely on charity schools to obtain any form of education. Portsea Beneficial School was a good example from the eighteenth century.

This page and opposite: The Treadgold Industrial Heritage Museum. Treadgolds of Portsea was established as an ironmonger's shop and smithy in Bishop Street in 1809 by William Treadgold, evolving over the years until final closure in 1988. For much of this period it was run as a family business, its site growing to encompass the remains of more than 20 different buildings erected between 1707 and 1866. Some of these buildings were early tenements, others were larger houses, yards, privies, stables, wash houses and the alleyways between. In the shop, ship's timbers were used in the ceiling construction including parts of an ancient cannonball rack. When trading ceased, Hampshire County Council purchased what was to be a unique piece of social and industrial history, a time warp still left with its contents of tools, equipment, metal supplies, domestic wares and ironmongery, much of which dated back over 100 years. The museum features many aspects of the business including the office, forge and workshop, stables, metal store, shop and stockroom just as they appeared on closure. At the rear a reconstructed tenement illustrates life when trading first started.

This page and opposite: Scenes at the newly-transformed Gunwharf Quays. The old Gunwharf site formed an important part of the naval dockyard and was originally constructed on reclaimed land in the early 1700s. It was built to store new and serviced guns prior to transportation to the ships and also to house shot and ordnance from vessels arriving for repair and refit. In 1919 the site was taken over as the naval torpedo school, the shore-established HMS *Vernon*, remaining here until closure in 1986. With some of the existing buildings recorded as scheduled ancient monuments and the entire site being declared a conservation area in 1992, planning permission was granted five years later for re-development of Gunwharf to a world-class waterfront by the Berkeley Group. The vision was to create a destination offering a wide range of shopping and leisure facilities together with new homes and berthing spaces capitalising on the superb location beside the busy harbour.

Much of the development is now complete and has proved to be an outstanding success with over 10 million visitors since the opening in March 2001. *Right:* The Grand Storehouse, the Vulcan Building, of 1811, being converted into residential apartments. *Bottom left:* The Isle of Wight car ferry to Fishbourne docking next to the development. *Bottom middle:* Enjoying the sunshine outside the Old Customs House, now a pub, which served as the main customs post of Portsmouth Harbour. The remaining phases of the development are anticipated to be completed in 2008.

The Spinnaker Tower is the new national landmark at the entrance to Portsmouth Harbour. The tower, which is currently being built beside Gunwharf Quays is the centre-piece of the £86 million Renaissance of Portsmouth Harbour project that is supported by £38 million from the Millennium Commission. Chosen by the people from three designs, the tower, when completed, will be 170m high and will feature viewing galleries reached by both an internal high-speed lift and an external glass panoramic lift. From the galleries superb views of the harbour and beyond for distances of at least 25 miles will be obtainable. As one of the most exciting and dramatic locations in the country and acting as the first British landmark visible for the millions of visitors now entering the United Kingdom on ships via Portsmouth Harbour, it is expected to draw even more visitors to the city itself. This photograph of the tower (left) , taken on the day after the top spire had been fitted, shows the structure almost complete.

Below: Part of the massive lower section of the tower.

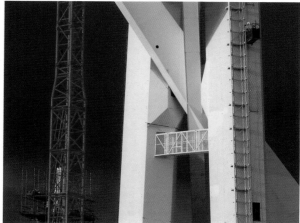

Already a dominant feature of Gunwharf Quays, the tower's construction has proved to be of great fascination to both residents and visitors who have watched the slow but steady progress of one of the most ambitious building projects in the country. Completion is expected during spring 2005 after this book has gone to press.

An almost timeless scene of late-Georgian Commercial Road in Landport. Charles Dickens' birthplace is in the far distance. It is hard to imagine that the busy M275 motorway access into the city is just a few metres from this point.

Nature takes over the Hilsea Lines. In 1757 the first defensive Lines were built south of Ports Creek to protect Portsea Island from an inland attack from the north. Reconstructed in 1858-60 to the formations that largely remain today, the Lines comprise a series of fortified bastions linked by massive earthworks overlooking a moat and stretch for over 2½ km along the whole northern side of the island. Later designated as a secondary line of defence to the Portsdown Hill fortifications to face the threat of a French invasion, they are now considerably overgrown, surrounded by trees and a haven for wildlife.

Above: A bricked-up gun port and ventilation shaft to the front face of the casemate of Bastion 3.

Left: The rear of the casemate of Bastion 6 at the eastern end of the lines.

Scenes and exhibits at Fort Nelson.

With the advent of rifled, breech loading, longer range artillery and renewed suspicions of Napoleon III's military ambitions, the whole of the Portsmouth defences were re-examined in a flurry of reports submitted during the 1850s to the Government. After many enquiries the decision was taken to construct a series of detached forts along the crest of Portsdown Hill as a first line of defence against any invasion from the north. These defences were to be supplemented by further fortifications along the Gosport Gomer/Elson line to the west, by the sea forts in the Solent and by considerable strength-ening of older fortifications already existing within the entire Portsmouth/Southampton/Isle of Wight areas. The whole project when completed formed a ring defence making Portsmouth one of the most heavily defended places in the world.

Since known as Palmerston's folly after the Prime Minister who sanctioned their construction, these works were built at the then enormous cost of some eleven million pounds and were some of the most extensive and costly fixed defences ever undertaken by Britain in peacetime. They featured the very latest thinking in military technology and yet such was the speed of progress that in a few years they were declared obsolete and never used in battle. The Portsdown Hill Forts comprising Forts Wallington, Nelson, Southwick, Widley and Purbrook along with the smaller Farlington and Crookhorn redoubts were finally completed in 1872 and all built to a generally similar polygonal design with dry moats flanked by caponiers. They incorporated both main and secondary armament along the ramparts and within and were designed to blend in with their surroundings when viewed from the north. The two redoubts have since been demolished but the five major forts still remain and have been put to various uses. The photographs on these two pages show different aspects of Fort Nelson, now the Royal Armouries collection of artillery and open to the public. *Above:* On-lookers await the live firing of the mid-day salute from the parade.

Spitbank Fort. Since the eastern approach of the Solent was considered to be too wide to be protected by shore batteries or a permanent barrier, four circular reinforced granite and armour-faced sea forts were constructed spaced across the water. Protecting the deep-water approach channels, the Spithead forts were built on shallow shoals and sandbanks using prepared stone and concrete ring foundations. Delays however were incurred due to political pressures, design changes and underwater constructional difficulties and although the works were started in 1865, the last fort was not finally completed until 1880. By this time any threatening situation had long since vanished!

Left: Looking down on to the central courtyard and well leading to the basement floor, Portsmouth and Southsea are in the far distance.

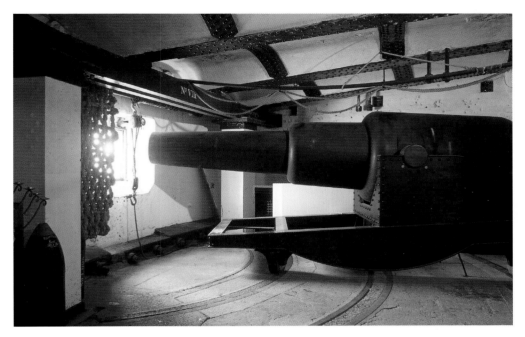

The larger Horse Sand and No Man's Land forts were built with two gun floors and a basement whilst the smaller Spitbank and St Helen's forts incorporated only one gun floor. Variously altered over the years, all the forts were still being used by the military until after the Second World War but since then all have been sold and are in private ownership. However, Spitbank Fort is now open to the general public and offers pub and party nights, Sunday lunches and can be booked for private functions. It is rightly described as the 'ultimate venue in the Solent' and since the fort has only been changed superficially since its original construction, the building still contains many fascinating period exhibits from its past history as shown here.

A view from the spit at Eastney looking over Langstone Harbour. The short ferry crossing to Hayling Island is just out of the picture to the right whilst Portsdown Hill is in the far distance. Due to its shallow waters, Langstone Harbour was unlikely to be used for any seaborne invasion and defences in this area east of Portsmouth were therefore kept to a minimum. However, the nearby low-lying Fort Cumberland, which was constructed under the direction of the Duke of Cumberland in 1746 and later rebuilt to defend the harbour entrance, has been described as one of the finest pieces of surviving defensive architecture in the country. With its star-shaped military geometry it is now owned by English Heritage and occasionally opened to the public. Within the harbour is one of the concrete caisson sections built for the D-Day Mulberry Harbour but never used.

The interior of Eastney Beam Engine House. Due to the enormous growth of population in the nineteenth century, the problems of Portsmouth's drainage were particularly acute, accentuated by the low-lying land form. It was only the provision of pumping stations and holding tanks to suit the tidal conditions at the principal outfall to Langstone Harbour that solved the dilemma. Eastney's 'high' engine house with its two massive James Watt steam-driven beam engines operating a series of pumps was opened in 1887. The pumps for each engine had a displacement of some 2¼ million litres per hour and with this installation the entire drainage system improved dramatically. Despite the more modern technology now used, the engines and house have survived and are open to the public on a regular basis administered by the Portsmouth Museum and Record Services.

It was reputed that at one time Portsmouth and Gosport had more pubs and drinking houses per square mile than any other town or city in the country. By the end of the eighteenth century there were over 250, a figure that rose almost fourfold during the next hundred or so years. In 1895 the Chancellor of the Exchequer told the Commons of a certain street containing 27 houses of which at least 16 were either public houses or licensed to sell alcohol. With Royal Navy crews spending long periods at sea, there was a tremendous demand for drinking and the then allied trade of prostitution on their return to port.

Reports in the 1860s warned the War Department of the 'temptations leading to intoxication and lust that are very great in Portsmouth'. A certain Reverend Smith in 1828 describing the flotilla of boats full of prostitutes or 'Solent nymphs' which met returning ships off Spithead and the scenes that followed as 'the opening of the bottomless pit'. It was only through the slow setting up of soldiers' and sailors' homes and institutes, provision of healthier recreational facilities on boats and on shore, stricter licensing laws with shorter opening hours and education generally that put an end to such events. Today the city has far fewer public houses but the photographs on these two pages act as a reminder of past times.

The church of St Mary, Kingston. The present church is the third church on this site, the original twelfth century medieval 'mother' church surviving until 1843 still surrounded by fields and farms. Its larger replacement designed by Thomas Ellis Owen, incorporated the tower of the original structure but by 1887 due to lack of light and ventilation it too was demolished. The church we now know was designed and constructed under the direction of Arthur Blomfield, the well-known Victorian church architect and generally regarded as his masterpiece. Built in Perpendicular Gothic style this spacious, soaring church in the words of Pevsner is 'intended to look and feel like the chief parish church of a great town'. It was completed in 1899 and in many ways is not dissimilar to the East Anglian wool churches. Both Isambard Kingdom Brunel, the famous engineer, and Charles Dickens were baptised in the original building.

The view from the top of the tower of St Mary's church gives an impression of the density of housing which covered most of Portsea Island during the nineteenth and early twentieth centuries. In the 1800s much of Portsea Island was still open farmland, by the end of the same century about three-quarters had been built on and by the Second World War virtually all was covered. Today the city is one of the most densely populated areas in Europe. The close terraced housing, laid out in a grid-iron fashion, is an interesting contrast to the winding tree-lined lanes of Thomas Ellis Owen's Southsea.

The Guildhall was designed by William Hill and completed in 1890. Built as the Landport Town Hall in an Italianate style reflecting late Victorian municipal pride, it became known as the Guildhall after 1926 when Portsmouth became a city. Most of the building was completely burnt out during a bombing raid in 1941 but later rebuilt within the original shell under the guidance of E. Berry Webber who retained most of the eastern frontage and side elevations. It was re-opened by H.M. Queen Elizabeth II in 1959.

The statue of Queen Victoria outside the civic offices was 'erected by public subscription during the mayoralty of Sir William T. Dupree and unveiled on July 8th 1903 by Lady Dupree'. On completion of the traffic-free Guildhall Square in 1972 it was moved to its present position directly facing the Guildhall. The statue is a striking feature of this central area of the city.

This page and opposite: Some of the exhibits within the Portsmouth City Museum, Art Gallery and Records Office. Situated within the north block of the old Clarence Barracks since 1972, the museum's principal features are evocative displays and settings showing local history under the title of *The story of Portsmouth* from Stone Age man through to the present day. Most aspects of the city, including its social and domestic life over the years, are shown and thematic temporary exhibitions are often held. There is a special gallery devoted to maritime art and local marine artists.

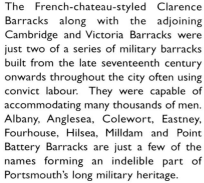

The French-chateau-styled Clarence Barracks along with the adjoining Cambridge and Victoria Barracks were just two of a series of military barracks built from the late seventeenth century onwards throughout the city often using convict labour. They were capable of accommodating many thousands of men. Albany, Anglesea, Colewort, Eastney, Fourhouse, Hilsea, Milldam and Point Battery Barracks are just a few of the names forming an indelible part of Portsmouth's long military heritage.

Part of the striking interior decoration to the Romanesque basilican church of St Agatha, Landport. Inspired by Father R. Dolling, a highly energetic Anglo/Catholic priest and designed by J. H. Ball, the church was completed in 1895, constructed in a slum district of narrow streets just outside the dockyard walls and closely hemmed in by housing. As a result it featured bare brick walling externally with windows generally at clerestory level only, there being no intention for the building to be viewed from public roads. In the Second World War, however, its parish was entirely destroyed by bombing and the church now sits in ungainly isolation surrounded by main roads and open spaces. Whilst the now exposed exterior is extremely plain, it is the magnificent internal decoration that makes the church outstanding artistically. Dolling wanted a building that could be beautified as time and funds allowed. In 1895, therefore, the artist Heywood Sumner was commissioned to start decoration work on the Lady Chapel, now demolished, followed by the chancel apse and semi-dome over. The subsequent murals were carried out in sgraffito, a technique involving the incision of lines in coloured plaster prior to setting which produces colours of great intensity and a clear definition of features. It is this work, now regarded as of international importance and one of Portsmouth's few major works of art, that make St Agatha's such a remarkable building. For a long time after the war, the church was closed and used as a naval store with the threat of demolition ever present. Fortunately, however, it has now been restored and open once again for services and as a gallery serving refreshments, its splendid decoration on view for all to see.

The New Theatre Royal. Remodelled from the original Theatre Royal in 1900 under the direction of John Walter Boughton and the classic theatre architect Frank Matcham, the enlarged building, the finest in the area, became an almost overnight success. With its striking iron balcony and decorative façade and with a stage which at one time was one of the largest in England, it has seen many fine performances by many of the country's greatest actors including Sarah Bernhardt, Henry Irving, Gladys Cooper, Sybil Thorndike and John Gielgud to name just a few. However, with the general loss of interest in theatres in the 1920s, the building was converted firstly to a cinema in 1932, back to a variety theatre in 1948 and after a brief period of closure, for use in 1960 as a Bingo Hall and finally for wrestling. Closure again came in 1966 and permission sought for demolition of a building then described as 'an eyesore on the centre of our fine city'. Fortunately this application was refused and in 1980 the building was purchased by the Theatre Royal Society. After considerable expenditure on repair and refurbishment, the New Theatre Royal is back in business, a great asset to the city and a credit to all concerned in its preservation.

Pompey in the news. Portsmouth Football Club was founded as a professional club in 1898 by a syndicate of sportsmen and businessmen. When the team first started playing, a sum of money was given to build a new stadium and ground named Fratton Park where the club still plays today and which on its completion was considered to be one of the finest grounds in England. The team initially played in pink and were known as 'the shrimps' and their first manager was Robert Brown retaining his position from 1911–1920 with a short stoppage during the years of the First World War. In 1939 the team won the FA cup final for the first time beating Wolverhampton Wanderers 4–1, to be followed by becoming football league champions in both 1948/49 and 1949/50 seasons. It was during this period that the legendary Jimmy Dickinson (Gentleman Jim) was playing for the club creating a record of 834 appearances and twice playing 100 consecutive league games in his twenty-year-long career. Like any other club, Portsmouth's fortunes have fluctuated considerably over the years but at the time of writing the team are sitting almost halfway up the Premiership League and the future looks promising.

The University of Portsmouth was inaugurated in 1992, its predecessor the former Portsmouth Polytechnic growing from the Portsmouth and Gosport School of Science and Arts originally founded in 1869. The University is now at the forefront of a rapidly changing, thriving city with its modern Guildhall Campus in the heart of the city and Langstone Campus on the edge of Langstone Harbour. The University takes a particular pride in its provision of a well structured and supportive learning environment and each year welcomes students from over 40 countries. A noticeable feature is the University's use of many interesting modern buildings often designed in striking fashion. Here the Guildhall Halls student accommodation building is shown reflected in the windows of University House.

Pound's Shipbreaking Yard. A familiar site from the M275 as one drives into or out of the city is Pound's Shipbreaking Yard on Tipner Point. Often seen with an elderly naval vessel being broken up, the family business of shipowners and shipbreakers has been in existence for many years. The site of the yard is shown on the 1811 edition of the Ordnance Survey map of the area as having a magazine built well away from all inhabitation of that time. The magazine was constructed around 1800 with room for some 24,000 barrels of gunpowder. The buildings that survive within Pound's yard today, whilst clearly intended originally for this purpose, may date from a slightly later period.

The view looking south over the inner reaches of Portsmouth Harbour from what is now the suburb of Paulsgrove. The Norman keep of Portchester Castle can be seen in the distance whilst on the left the apartments and flats mark the entrance to Port Solent Marina. The Thames sailing barge *Kitty* can also be seen moored outside the entrance and is available for sailing charters

This page and opposite: Port Solent is one of the south coast's leading leisure attractions. Featuring the third largest marina in the UK and a considerable number of up-market shops, retail outlets, bars, pubs, restaurants, with a cinema and leisure club, it has a distinctly Mediterranean atmosphere along its boardwalks. On hot summer days there is the feeling of being transported to a far distant port, yet much of the development has been built on reclaimed land within the harbour.

Boats swing idly at anchor with the umbrella-shaded boardwalks or luxury apartments behind.

Scenes in Commercial Road. By the end of the nineteenth century Landport had become the commercial and administrative centre of Portsea Island as illustrated by its new Town Hall later to become the Guildhall. Commercial Road grew into the main shopping centre and still retains that position. Almost completely destroyed by bombing, the shopping centre was rebuilt after the war notably using Portland stone for most of the main façades and was pedestrianised in the 1970s. The fountain at the junction with Arundel Street was given by Allders to commemorate the Queen's Silver Jubilee of 1977.

The Cascades Shopping Centre opened in 1989 with its main entrance from Commercial Road. The centre occupies an area that was previously used as a car park situated at the rear of two of the largest stores in the city. Prior to the Second World War bombing it had been housing. Now the largest indoor shopping centre in Portsmouth and described as a whole High Street under one roof, the Cascades is always busy and thronged with local shoppers. This view is taken looking across the food court with Christmas decorations in considerable evidence!

'It's shorter by water' with the Gosport Ferry. Acting as a frequent waterbus between both sides of the harbour, the ferry operates continuously throughout the daytime and evenings taking only a few minutes for each journey. The two communities have been closely knit for many hundreds of years, their principal common interest being the interchange of workforce in the service of the Navy and military. There has been a ferry service here since the reign of Queen Elizabeth I. Records exist of individual boatmen who would row passengers and animals across the mouth of the harbour for as little as one penny, rising to sixpence during rough weather! A floating bridge began operating in 1840 but since 1959 conventional ferries have been working the crossing. A planned super-tram system with a tunnel beneath the water is at present still under consideration. In the background the spectacular rising Spinnaker Tower, the Gunwharf Quays development and The Hard Interchange with Portsmouth Harbour railway station can be seen.

Over the Water
GOSPORT

Part of the newly landscaped Gosport waterfront near the ferry landing stage. The masts of HMS *Victory* and *Warrior* can be seen rising amongst the dockyard buildings across the harbour. The decorative mosaic rondel in the foreground at the entrance to Falklands Gardens has the wording 'In dedication to those who bravely left these shores to serve in the D-Day Landings of 1944 and the Falkland Islands Conflict in 1982' inset around it.

Originally a fishing village, Gosport started to grow during the early 1600s into a small town situated on the west bank of the harbour immediately opposite Old Portsmouth and the naval dockyard. By the 1670s it had been enclosed with a moat and ramparts in a similar manner to Portsmouth, these being gradually enlarged and rebuilt for the expanding town, improved defence and the military's requirements over the next one hundred or so years. However, by the mid-nineteenth century Gosport had sprawled haphazardly beyond its ramparts, its growth only being held in check by the Palmerston line of fortifications between Gomer and Elson. Since then the town has increased still further engulfing the old villages of Alverstoke and Rowner, joining up with Fareham along the busy A32 and leaving only a narrow strip of open countryside between it and the resorts of Lee-on-the-Solent and Stubbington. Gosport's 800th birthday was celebrated in 2004.

Gosport's pedestrianised High Street. Like Portsmouth, much of Gosport's old town was destroyed by bombing during the Second World War and the subsequent rebuilding afterwards. At one time the town would have been heavily congested behind its ramparts with three main parallel streets linked by alleyways and narrow thoroughfares. Of the old housing left in Gosport, this row towards the end of the High Street is generally regarded as the finest. Recently pedestrianised, the High Street now hosts a twice-weekly market with many hundreds of stalls — the largest on the south coast.

The interior of the parish church of the Holy Trinity. Originally built as a chapel of ease to Alverstoke in the late seventeenth century and enlarged in 1734, the church was extensively restored in 1887 with its campanile being added two years later. However, internally the nave with its two rows of columns, each worked from a single oak trunk, and semi-circular apse are those of the original building almost untouched and a striking contrast with what one would expect from the exterior. The great treasure of the church is the organ on which Handel played, originally at Stanmore where he was organist to the Duke of Chandos. The organ was brought to Gosport in the mid eighteenth century. The campanile is now a notable Gosport landmark in an area completely re-developed with the church acting as the central feature.

Below: Near the station is a short section of old railway line leading through to the former Royal Clarence Yard and Queen Victoria's private station, adjacent to Clarence Pier. Here the Queen would alight for the crossing by Royal Yacht to the Isle of Wight. This mosaic paving panel, at the point where the line crosses Weevil Lane and passes into the yard, has the words 'Queen Victoria's funeral train passed here from Royal Clarence Yard accompanied by the King, the Kaiser and numerous royalty'.

Above: The derelict shell of Gosport railway station. Opened in 1842 by the London & South Western Railway as the terminus of the then important branch line from Eastleigh via Fareham, the line not only served Gosport but also Portsmouth in conjunction with the passenger ferry across the harbour. It was not until five years later that Portsmouth was connected directly to the railway network.

The main features of the station building are its single storey construction and 14-pillared colonnade on the south side. The height of the building was dictated by the necessity of retaining field of fire for the guns on the nearby town ramparts. Passenger services ceased in 1953 followed by cessation of freight traffic in 1969 by which time war damage and fire had destroyed the overall roof leaving its historic façade, dating back to the dawn of the railway age, still intact. The building's future is still being assessed for possible use within the proposed South East Hampshire Light Rapid Transport Link.

Fishing is a popular recreation on the new Haslar Marina Millennium Pier opened in 2001 with its superb views across the water to Old Portsmouth. The pier is another aspect of the newly restored waterfront under the Renaissance of Portsmouth Harbour Scheme. The nearby marina was built to cope with the large demand for berths in the Solent and can hold nearly 700 boats. The old Trinity House Lightship acts as the marina's clubhouse. P & O ferry *Pride of Le Havre* is seen here entering the harbour.

The Royal Navy Submarine Museum occupies part of the former submarine base of HMS *Dolphin* at Haslar. Here visitors can experience 100 years of submarines at the cradle of the most powerful of Britain's fighting forces. The museum features many aspects of the country's submarine service, its weaponry and life below the waves. The Royal Navy's first submarine, *Holland I*, is on display and visitors can enjoy walk-through guided tours of HMS *Alliance* shown here. Nearby, the 30m submarine escape training tower at Fort Blockhouse is visible from the Museum.

Opposite page: The Royal Hospital Haslar was built on a 40 hectare site between 1746 and 1762 and at the time of its construction was described as the largest red brick building in Europe. Originally intended to be quadrangular in form with each side consisting of a double row of buildings about 170m long, only three sides were built ultimately, the south-west face being omitted. Constructed due to the urgent need for medical care for sick and hurt seamen of the Georgian Navy, the hospital by the end of the eighteenth century was treating between 1500 and 2000 patients in its 84 wards at any one time. Since many of these patients would have been 'pressed' into the Navy against their will, the hospital was also designed to prevent their escape and as such acted as a prison with high iron railings and guards posted at the weak points such as entrances and sewerage outlets! Accommodation for administrative officers and surgeons was also built along with church, laundry, dispensary and other associated requirements. One wing was set aside as a 'lunatic asylum' for men driven mad by the hardships of naval life and warfare and the poor souls routinely subjected to brutal treatment in their 'best interests'. Over the years many additional buildings and facilities have been added and Haslar has treated the sick and wounded from every major conflict from the Napoleonic Wars to the Falklands War. Civilians are now also admitted and the hospital has acted in recent years as a district general hospital for the Gosport area. Government plans considering the closure of Haslar on financial grounds have met with much local opposition but clearly the future of the hospital is now in grave doubt.

Right: The main façade of the north-east quadrangular block. *Below:* All that remains of a tramway which originally ran from Haslar Jetty, where patients were off-loaded, up and into the main hospital buildings.

Left: 'The Terrace' built in 1798 as accommodation for senior officers and their families. *Above:* An overgrown memorial in the Garden of Remembrance. There are many thousands of bodies buried here, laid to rest over some 250 years.

The 'Explosion' Museum of Naval Firepower is situated at the historic former Royal Navy armament depot on Priddy's Hard and tells the story of naval warfare from the eighteenth century to the Gulf War. The lives of the munitions workers are also described in detail and the museum possesses a unique collection of small arms, cannons and guns, shells and munitions, mines, torpedoes and modern missiles. An audio-visual show is presented in the original 'grand' gunpowder magazine of 1771 once capable of storing almost 200,000kg of gunpowder within its 2½m thick buttressed brick walls and now the building around which the museum is based. Priddy's Hard, originally an isolated shore of some 40 hectares opposite the dockyard was purchased in 1758 to store and supply gunpowder to the wooden sailing ships and later munitions and weapons to the modern Navy until its closure in 1989. These photographs show a few different aspects of the museum.

A view across the inner reaches of the harbour from near Hardway. Hardway, originally known as Widhay, is an ancient village with its origins dating back to the Roman conquest. Historical evidence points to a connection with Portchester Castle and trade between villagers and the occupying Romans. For hundreds of years Hardway was isolated from Gosport by Forton Creek making it an ideal location for smuggling. Old maps indicate 'hards' from which goods and passengers loaded and unloaded including convicts bound for transportation ships from 'convict's' hard. As nearby Priddy's Hard slowly developed from the mid eighteenth century, Hardway began to grow and communications were laid down. In both World Wars the waters and foreshore of Hardway were heavily used for re-fuelling and repairs to naval vessels and much equipment and personnel for the D-Day landings embarked from here. Today the waters are quieter, favoured by yachtsmen and overlooked by newly developed housing and apartments.

Fort Brockhurst. Amongst the mid-nineteenth century proposals for further fortifications around the Portsmouth region, later to be known as Palmerston's folly, and described earlier, were three new forts to be built between the existing Forts Gomer and Elson. The five were in an almost straight inner line straddling the entire Gosport peninsular and acted as a defence against any attack from the west. Additional proposals were also made for a Gosport outer or advanced line to be positioned between Fareham and Lee-on-the-Solent but only Fort Fareham was ever built. Construction of the three new forts of the inner line, Forts Grange, Rowner and Brockhurst commenced around 1860 and with their wet surrounding ditches and self-contained 'keeps of last resort', they differed notably in design from the Portsdown Hill fortifications. Today Forts Grange, Rowner and Elson are still in use by the services, Gomer has been demolished but Fort Brockhurst, very little altered since its original construction, has been designated an Ancient Monument and is now in the care of English Heritage, who at certain times open it to the general public.

The refurbished and restored crescent at Alverstoke. Designed by Thomas Ellis Owen, this is the only Regency crescent in Hampshire and was completed about 1825. It was intended to be the centrepiece of a new marine town called Anglesyville or Anglesea, a watering place to rival Bath or Brighton as a fashionable resort but, due to financial difficulties, the scheme was abandoned and the crescent never completed. The gardens opposite were an integral part of the crescent facilities together with a reading room and two bathhouses, sadly now demolished. However, with great foresight by both the local authority and the crescent residents, the gardens have recently been restored to their Georgian splendour and planted with authentic plants and shrubs of the period. Alverstoke itself is mentioned in the Domesday Book, a small farming community that has only in the last hundred or so years been slowly engulfed by the spread of neighbouring Gosport.

High summer on Southsea beach with South Parade Pier in the background. Many hotels and boarding houses of the nineteenth century widely advertised the beach's south-facing aspect and views and their own facilities of 'certified sanitation, hot water sea baths and spacious coffee and sitting rooms'. The telegrams to the Royal Beach Hotel were simply to be addressed to 'sunshine'!

Resort within a City
SOUTHSEA

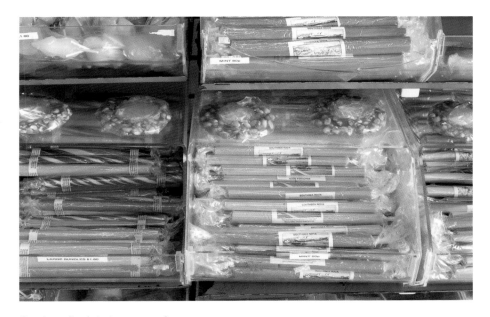

Southsea Rock in its many colours.

In the 1850s Southsea was described by a contemporary observer as 'a sort of compromise between a fortified place and a watering place'. Professional and officer families felt the need to escape from the crowded confines of Old Portsmouth and the new speculative developments to the rear of Southsea Common resolved their dilemma. Once known as the Great Morass, this area of marsh and scrub was steadily being reclaimed and increasingly built upon, often in a haphazard fashion and by 1900 most of the area had been covered, only the common itself being kept clear, initially for military needs.

Sea bathing was enhanced by a sloping shingle beach into deep water encouraged by an ever increasing number of bathing machines. Southsea not only offered a mild climate but also the spectacle of magnificent sea views to the Isle of Wight and, on regular occasions, the fleet reviews off Spithead, sometimes featuring mock naval engagements. As a result excursionists began to arrive in their thousands and the resort within a city was born. The presence of the Royal Navy was undoubtedly one of the resort's great selling points and the arrival of the railway, first to Portsmouth in 1847 and later to Southsea itself in 1885, greatly increased the flow of visitors and prospective property purchasers.

Long before Southsea was to become a resort it was realised that the area also had considerable defensive possibilities. Under a decree by Henry VIII in 1544 and as part of a programme to update the 'Saxon Shore' forts, Southsea Castle was built. Situated at the extreme tip of Portsea Island, it guarded the deep-water approach to Portsmouth Harbour. With its square stone keep in a surrounding bailey yard, elevated gun positions on the outer wall encircled by a dry moat and angled bastions, it was built to the latest design in defence thinking. It was from the castle that Henry VIII watched his ships in an engagement in the Solent with the French in 1545 and the subsequent sinking of the pride of the English fleet, the *Mary Rose*. Over the years many modifications and considerable reconstruction have been carried out to update its defensive capabilities and a lighthouse was built on the western gun platform in the 1820s. Finally in 1960 the castle was acquired by the City Council, who have restored the building to its nineteenth-century appearance and re-opened it as a museum.

Two of the displays within the castle's keep. There are many exhibits featured not only regarding the castle but also more generally covering the defences of Portsmouth. In summer civil war re-enactments take place and facilities exist for the building to be used for both private and civil functions.

Thomas Ellis Owen's Southsea. Features of Netley Terrace, Queen's Terrace and Swiss Cottage.

Thomas Ellis Owen was born in 1805, growing up to join his architect father initially in designing churches, followed by the elegant crescent at Alverstoke. In 1834 he began to design and speculatively build villas and terraces in Southsea to suit the growing demands for property outside Old Portsmouth's walls. This work continued for at least twenty years, many of the designs almost certainly being influenced by John Nash's developments around Regent's Park in London. During this period much of Southsea was still open common and countryside and Owen's developments were mainly confined to the Kent Road, Sussex Road, Sussex Place, Queen's Place and Portland Road areas. In Southsea altogether about 160 houses are attributed to Owen, many featuring classical and Gothic architecture in romantic landscaped settings. Thomas Ellis Owen has accordingly often been described as the maker of modern Southsea. *Above:* A curvy lane leads to Sussex Terrace completed in 1855.

South Parade Pier has had a somewhat chequered history, the present structure being the third design on the site. The first pier, designed by George Rake, was opened in 1879 and contained a small concert hall at its extremity. Unfortunately the pier had only a short life and most of the structure was destroyed by fire in 1904. Its replacement was completed four years later under the direction of George Smith. It was built in a much grander style accommodating a large concert hall, tea rooms, shops, bandstand and pavilion capable of seating an audience of over two thousand. It was described as both a summer pleasure pier and winter palace and was highly popular with visitors over many years. Sadly, having survived the war another fire broke out in 1974 during the filming of 'Tommy' that totally gutted the Edwardian interior, necessitating the rebuilding to its present day form. Despite its somewhat truncated appearance and fewer facilities, the pier is still a major attraction and any warm summer weekend will find its deck thronged with visitors.

A busy summer's day looking along the seafront to South Parade Pier. With its wide traffic-free promenade this is an ideal place for strolling, jogging or just watching the world go by at any time of the year from one of the several cafés along its length. The Solent Way footpath passes along the whole of Southsea front.

Today's colourful Clarence Pier built in 1961 now forms part of the amusement park at the western end of Clarence Esplanade. It replaces Southsea's very first pier the Clarence Esplanade Pier which opened one hundred years earlier. The original pier was built initially as a landing stage for steamers but was soon discovered by the rapidly increasing number of the resort's visitors. It became so popular that gatekeepers were employed to segregate the gentry from the 'riff-raff' along its deck. However, its fortunes were not to last. In the 1870s the combination of the new harbour railway station, attracting the Isle of Wight ferries, and the opening of the South Parade Pier, started a slow but steady decline. In 1941 an air-raid abruptly and finally destroyed it.

Chips with everything! South Parade Pier beyond.

Colour, colour everywhere. A selection of Southsea seafront souvenirs.

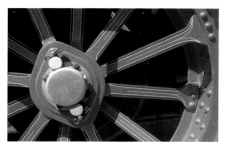

This page and opposite: Scenes at the annual Portsmouth and Southsea Show held on Southsea Common. Providing a mix of entertainment including demonstrations, crafts, flower and horticultural displays, exhibitions, pet shows, circus, features by local societies, agricultural matters, fairground, vintage steam engines, numerous catering, sales and trade outlets and stands, the show is an extremely popular three day event. Much of it is held under a series of large marquees in case of inclement weather but in general terms it seems to be an event that brings out the sunshine in every sense of the word.

With its large open space Southsea Common is an ideal venue for such events and throughout the year hosts all manner of shows, exhibitions, displays and concerts.

Floating apparitions at the annual Kite Festival. It was only the needs of the Army keeping the common clear of speculative development during the nineteenth century that provided Southsea with this outstanding feature today. Adjacent to beach and promenade, this long open space stretching east from the limits of Old Portsmouth and on past South Parade Pier is noted for its superb floral displays, its facilities for bowls, cricket, croquet, golf, putting, skating, tennis and provision of a large boating lake.

Aspects of Southsea. Palmerston Road pedestrianised shopping centre with the church of St Jude beyond designed by Thomas Ellis Owen; the Canoe Lake adjacent to Southsea Esplanade; a bowls match in progress; the Queen's Hotel opened in 1861; looking across the lawns to South Parade and nineteenth century housing in Great Southsea Street.

Lest we forget. Poignant symbols of remembrance at the Royal Naval War Memorial on Southsea Common.

The memorial was designed by Sir Robert Lorimer and unveiled in 1924 to commemorate the 9666 Portsmouth-based sailors who died in the First World War. The later walled extension with its two pavilions on the monument's landward side commemorates the 14,797 sailors and marines who died in the Second World War and who 'have no grave but the sea'.

The seafront features many other memorials from past conflicts and imperial forays, some of which have been moved from different parts of the city due to road or building developments. Amongst these are reminders of the fallen during the Indian Mutiny, the Crimean War and the Battle of Trafalgar. There are memorials to those who died in the nineteenth century whilst serving with HMS *Aboukir*, HMS *Trident* and HMS *Chesapeake* and it is these, together with the various statues of military personalities, that bring home the long history of this naval city.

The D-Day sixtieth anniversary commemorations. Veterans march past along Southsea Esplanade on Sunday 6 June 2004 after a commemoration service at the D-Day stone, organised by the Royal British Legion. Many hundreds of on-lookers took part in the service and watched the parade after, the salute being taken by Her Majesty's Lord Lieutenant of Hampshire, Mrs Mary Fagan.

Worn with pride. Medals carried by some of the veterans taking part in the Southsea commemorations.

Visitors queue outside the D-Day Museum during the sixtieth anniversary weekend of the allied landings.

The D-Day Museum was opened in 1984 to commemorate D-Day 40 and extended ten years later. Its many displays take the visitor through the build up to D-Day (Operation Overlord), the day of the Allied invasion of Normandy on 6 June 1944 and its context within the Second World War. There are also other more general features of the sights and sounds of Britain at war with film shows using original historic footage and archive film.

The museum's centrepiece is the magnificent Overlord Tapestry commissioned by Lord Dulverton as a tribute to the sacrifice and heroism of those men and women who took part in Operation Overlord. The tapestry, designed by Sandra Lawrence, is 83m long and the longest work of its kind in the world, conceived as a modern counterpart to the Bayeux Tapestry. *Above:* A scene from the tapestry showing flotillas of Royal Navy minesweepers clearing channels ahead of the main invasion force.

This page and opposite: **All eyes on Portsmouth.** Crowds enjoy the sunshine and an open-air concert featuring the Glenn Miller Orchestra UK on Southsea Castle field on Sunday 6 June 2004.

A D-Day sixtieth anniversary floral display on Southsea Common with the housing of Clarence Parade beyond. The many floral displays and beds along the seafront and common at Southsea are a notable feature throughout the year and much admired by residents and visitors alike. The rose garden situated within the remains of Lumps Fort is a sanctuary for those seeking a little peace and quiet away from the busier areas of the resort.

Part of the Memorial Garden at the Royal Marines Museum situated in the old Eastney Barracks at the far eastern end of the seafront. Behind is a section of the barrack's long centre block built in the 1860s and once used as the marines' quarters.

The barracks were closed in 1991 but the museum, founded a few years later, is housed within the old officers' mess, described as one of the most stately of its type in England. Among the many scenes and items of military history on display which tell the story of the Royal Marines is one of the most comprehensive collections of medals in the world covering awards for gallantry and service.

The Memorial Garden, opened by Prince Philip in 1995, features many tributes to past conflicts and the stones shown here were taken from areas of the Two Sisters and Mount Harriet in the Falkland Islands. Selected and donated by the islanders, they have been erected here in memory of those Royal Marines who fell in the Falklands War in 1982.

The auditorium of the King's Theatre. The King's Theatre was the brainchild of John Walter Boughton, who had earlier taken over the Portsmouth Theatre Company at the New Theatre Royal. By employing one of the greatest theatre architects Frank Matcham, he created what is now regarded as one of the best examples of the Edwardian playhouse to be found in Britain. Opened in 1907 with its Italian Renaissance style of décor, it has seen performances by practically all the great names of the English stage and in recent times has had many 'prior to London' productions. In 2001, after a campaign to keep the theatre open, it was purchased by Portsmouth City Council. In almost 100 years the theatre has changed very little apart from essential updating of facilities and considerable refurbishment. Dame Sybil Thorndike always loved to act at 'the King's' because of, 'the wonderful appreciation of the warm-hearted audience of Portsmouth'.

A replica of an *Iguanodon* welcomes visitors to the Portsmouth Natural History Museum situated off Eastern Parade. In this relatively small building the museum's displays aim to celebrate the diversity of life in and around Portsmouth. The exhibits take the visitor on a journey through the wild places of Portsmouth present and Portsmouth past. These range from mudflats, marshes, seashore and woodland to grassland and built-up areas of the city. The forming of the earth, the geology of Hampshire, the grasslands of Portsdown Hill, the woodlands of the Hilsea Lines, the Farlington Marshes and the urban desert – all feature here. In addition the heated butterfly house filled with exotic living insects and plants is always popular with children.

Left: The hovercraft service to Ryde on the Isle of Wight has proved to be an extremely efficient method for reaching the island. The crossing, starting at Clarence Esplanade slipway, takes just under ten minutes and has now been in operation for over thirty years. The service is fast, frequent and reliable and runs throughout the year. Here onlookers watch one of the craft turning, ready to depart on its short journey across the Solent.

Right: A plaque near the hovercraft terminal celebrates the homecoming of Sir Alex Rose and his landing on Southsea beach on the 4 July 1968 after his single-handed circumnavigation of the globe in his yacht *Lively Lady*.

A late winter's afternoon looking across the waters of Spithead to the Isle of Wight. Spitbank Fort is silhouetted on the left. A view that must have been seen by countless generations of sailors and travellers as they arrived or departed to and from this great naval city over the last two thousand or so years.

High summer looking from Portsdown Hill northwards over ripening fields. Beyond is the wooded greenery of some of the remaining fragments of the ancient Forest of Bere, at one time stretching in a great arc from King's Somborne in the west to Rowlands Castle in the east. It was here the Saxon kings would go hunting, long before the Normans made it a Royal Forest. Portsdown Hill forming the city's northern boundary acts as a great divide between the urban and the rural.

THE COUNTRYSIDE

The tiny secluded Saxon church of St Nicholas at Boarhunt lies in a fold of the northern slope of Portsdown Hill. Surrounded by woods and fields and by isolated farms and cottages, its situation is totally rural despite the close proximity of Portsmouth to the south of the hill. The building has been dated to about 1064 and appears to have no later structural modifications apart from its bell turret. Over the short distance from city to church, time can revert back almost 1000 years.

This page and opposite: The village of Southwick also lies near Portsdown Hill. Still mostly a private estate, the village has remained remarkably free from suburban development despite its easy access to and from the city and presents a delightful collection of domestic architecture ranging back over several centuries. The nearby Southwick House incorporated within the HMS *Dryad* school of navigation became the headquarters of Admiral Sir Bertram Ramsay, the allied naval Commander-in-Chief for the invasion of Nazi-occupied Europe in 1944, and contains the famous D-Day map room now open to visitors. Generals Eisenhower and Montgomery were quartered here and the Operation Overloard sign outside the Golden Lion public house *(opposite)* records this historical period and their drinking preferences. *Above:* A scene from the annual Southwick village show with Morris dancing in progress.

The dedication of the village church of 'St James-without-the-Priory Gate' refers back to the time when an Augustinian Priory was established here between 1145 and 1153. The church, described as 'The Peculiar of Southwick' is exempt from diocesan and other jurisdiction by ancient privilege although it still strictly adheres to the doctrine and order of the Church of England.

OPERATION OVERLORD

In the days leading up to the invasion of Normandy, "D-Day", on the 6th June 1944, the Saloon Bar of The Golden Lion Public House, Southwick was taken over as an unofficial Officers Mess.

In those days the present bar consisted of two rooms, the front being known as The Blue Room and the one at the rear, The Gold Room. These were so named by the Officers to reflect the colour of the decorations and furnishings.

Some years on, the barmaid who served at the house in 1944 still resides in the village as we have therefore her confirmation that General Dwight D.Eisenhower drank half pints of bitter here, whilst General Sir Bernard Montgomery confined himself to grapefruit juice.

The beer dispensed to the General was brewed in the brewhouse at the rear of this property.

Autumn in the beech woods of the Queen Elizabeth Country Park. The park, the largest in Hampshire, contains 564 hectares of wood and downland and is jointly managed by Hampshire County Council and Forest Enterprise. It is an extremely popular location for walkers, cyclists and horse riding and has many footpaths, tracks and easy access to the adjacent South Downs Way.

Butser Hill is situated within the park and at 270m is one of the highest points on the South Downs. This view from near its summit looks towards the village of East Meon in the distance. Charles Dickens, in *Nicholas Nickleby* described the hill and its surroundings as 'there shot up, almost perpendicularly into the sky, a height so steep as to hardly be accessible to any but the sheep and goats that fed upon its sides, and there, stood a mound of green, sloping and tapering off so delicately, and merging so gently into the level ground, that you could scarce define its limits. Hills swelling above each other; and undulations, shapely and uncouth, smooth and rugged, graceful and grotesque, thrown negligently side by side, bounded the view in each direction'.

A view looking east across Farlington Marshes local nature reserve. The reserve is the largest open space in Portsmouth and a site of international importance for birds that visit and pass through to and from places as far apart as eastern Canada, Siberia and southern Africa. Over 200 bird species have been recorded on the marshes. The costs of running the reserve by Hampshire Wildlife Trust are drawn from funds raised by its membership of over 11,000 and by donations and grants.

Gales Brewery, Horndean. George Gale & Co Ltd is Hampshire's leading family brewery, having been founded in Horndean by Richard Gale in 1847. Originally located in the Ship and Bell Inn, the brewery was re-built on its present site next door in 1869 under the direction of Richard's youngest son George, by then Master Brewer. In 1896 the brewery was sold to the Bowyer family from Guildford who still own the business. Gales Brewery possesses over 100 public houses throughout Hampshire, Berkshire, Surrey and Sussex and is best known for its HSB beer, first produced in 1959, together with a range of other award-winning traditional cask-conditioned beers and old country wines. Conducted tours can be arranged around the brewery during most days of the year.

Part of the mural discovered in 1864 on the north wall of the chancel of St Hubert's chapel at Idsworth. The mural is thought to have been painted around 1330 and is unusual for its completeness and quality. Divided into two sections by a horizontal zig-zag patterned band, it is generally agreed that the lower panel depicts the presentation of the head of St John the Baptist on a salver to Salome at King Herod's feast. The upper section shows a hunting scene that has been subject to various interpretations over the years.

The ancient chapel of St Hubert was built in the mid eleventh century probably under the direction of Godwin, Earl of Wessex and premier Earl of England. It may well have been constructed on the foundations of a much earlier building. Standing alone near the Sussex border, shown here surrounded by spring fields, the chapel has escaped the ravages of Victorian 'restoration' and is a haven of peace, calm and simplicity.

Wickham has been described by Pevsner in his *Buildings of England* as the finest village in Hampshire and one of the best in the south of England. Built around a large rectangular 'square', its many buildings present an outstanding variety of architectural styles and materials in a scale sympathetic with the village's layout and space.

This page and opposite: Groups of images showing a few of the many styles and architectural details to be found, ranging from early Georgian to the twentieth century.

At one time the village had a charter for a market and fair in the 1260s and it was possibly for this reason that the square was laid out. There is little doubt that many of the houses are much older than they appear from the front, having been re-faced during succeeding periods of architectural fashion. Wickham owes its existence to the River Meon, many of the village's former industries harnessing water power including the old brewery and tannery.

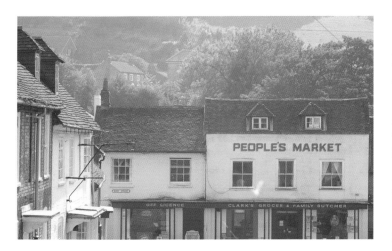

Aspects of Hambledon. Once a market town in the Middle Ages, it declined to village status by the eighteenth century and the 'people's market' wording over shops in West Street *(left)* acts as a reminder of former glories. Hambledon became the first major centre in the country for serious cricket with its Hambledon Cricket Club playing on the nearby Broadhalfpenny Down since the eighteenth century. Cricket's early history seems to be particularly associated with the Downs of Hampshire, Kent and Sussex. Records exist of a form of the game played by pupils of Winchester College in the 1640s with other forms probably played on numerous other grounds as well. However, it is the name of Hambledon that has a particularly important place in the game's pioneering years with the present day rules being laid down by the club in 1774.

The sign outside the Bat and Ball public house overlooking Broadhalfpenny Down gives a clear indication of cricket in its formative years. *(Below left.)*

The ruins of the Premonstratensian Abbey at Titchfield. Founded by Peter des Roches, Bishop of Winchester in 1232, it is the last house of this order to be founded in England. After the dissolution, the abbey was converted into a mansion by the Earl of Southampton and the great gatehouse, which today dominates the site, built in the remains of the nave of the monastic church and completed by 1542. After being occupied by many generations, the house was largely demolished in the 1780s, some of the salvaged materials being used to restore Cams Hall in Fareham. Only the shell of the Tudor gatehouse shown here remains virtually intact.

Looking west along the beach at Lee-on-the-Solent towards Southampton. Lee began to grow as a seaside health resort in the late nineteenth century, its branch railway from Fort Brockhurst and Fareham opening in 1884 and its pier in 1885. Both railway and pier have now gone but with a high sunshine record, glorious views across the Solent to the Isle of Wight and its convenient location for access to both Portsmouth and Southampton, the resort is still growing.

A final brief and famous comment from Nelson himself!

PHOTOGRAPHIC CREDITS

All photographs taken by and © Iain McGowan FRPS except for the following:

Board of Trustees of the Armouries/Iain McGowan, pp64, 65; Pete Bamforth, p58 (bottom right); Toby Chappell, the King's Theatre, p124; the Mary Rose Trust, p48; Pat Mitchell, p51; the Portsmouth City Museums, p69; the Portsmouth City Museums/Overlord Embroidery Trust, p119; POA (phot) Gary Davies 2SL photographer, p42; Tony Tracy, rear cover; Joy Whiting, p116.

ACKNOWLEDGEMENTS

I would like to thank the many people who have helped me in the compilation of this book by loaning photographs, allowing photography, being photographed, providing information, advising on or contributing to captions and offering technical support. I am therefore most grateful to the following:-

Pete Bamforth; Eric Birbeck and Surgeon Captain James Campbell RN (Royal Hospital Haslar); Nigel Chapman; David Culverwell; Chris Dobbs (Mary Rose Trust); Sarah Eastall (English Heritage); The Revd Karina Green (St George's church, Portsea); Nicholas Hall (Royal Armouries – Fort Nelson); Ann Lee; Fr. John Maunder (St Agatha's church); Pat Mitchell; Linda and Patrick Pead; Harry Pounds (Pounds Shipowners and Shipbreakers); Paul Raymond (Portsmouth Museums and Records Services); Neil Rowe (St Ann's church, Royal Naval Dockyard); Jacquie Shaw (Portsmouth Historic Dockyard); Jenny Stilling (Cascades Shopping Centre); Simon Smith (Royal Naval Dockyard); Tony Tracy; Robin Tucker and Ian Pratt (King's Theatre, Southsea); Sylvia and Jim Waddington; the Revd Canon Bob White (St Mary's church, Kingston); the Curators and staff at the Eastney Pumping Station; the Explosion Museum of Naval Firepower; the Portsmouth City Museum, Art Gallery and Records Office; the Portsmouth Natural History Museum; the Royal Armouries – Fort Nelson; the Royal Navy Submarine Museum; Portchester Castle; Southsea Castle and Gales Brewery.

In particular I wish to thank Joy once again for her patience, support and hard work in typing the manuscript, Steven Pugsley and his colleagues at Halsgrove Ltd for their commission and assistance throughout the project and finally fellow photographer Roger Holman for that initial introduction.

REFERENCE SOURCES

There are numerous books, booklets, papers, leaflets and guides about Portsmouth, Gosport, Southsea and the surrounding district. It is an almost impossible task to mention them all but the following have been invaluable as reference sources:

Arlott, J, *From Hambledon to Lords,* Barry Shurlock, 1975

Bardell, M, *History and guide: Portsmouth,* Tempus Publishing, 2001

Broadbent, G, *Portsmouth and the South Coast – A Guide to the Region,* The News/PCC, 1999

Brown, R, *The Pubs of Portsmouth,* Milestone Publications, 1984

Brown, R, *Gosport's Pictorial Past,* Milestone Publications, 1983

Corney, A, *Fortifications in Old Portsmouth,* Portsmouth City Museums, 1965

Defoe, D, *A Tour Through the Whole Island of Great Britain,* 1724

Easthope, W, *Smitten City,* The Evening News

Hamilton Ellis, C, *The London Brighton and South Coast Railway,* Ian Allan, 1960

Hamilton Ellis, C, *The London and South Western Railway,* George Allen and Unwin, 1956

Hubbuck, R, *Portsmouth Papers No 8 – Portsea Island Churches,* PCC, 1976

Mason, P and Harrison, J, *Hampshire – A Sense of Place,* Hampshire Books, 1994

Mitchell, G and Cantwell, A and Sprack, P, *Solent Papers No.1 – Spit Bank and the Spithead Forts,* David Moore, 2003

Mitchell, G and Cobb, P, *Solent Papers No.3 – Fort Nelson and the Portsdown Forts,* David Moore, 1987

Ordnance Survey, *Explorer Map 119; Meon Valley, Portsmouth, Gosport and Fareham*

Pevsner, N and Lloyd, D, *The Buildings of England: Hampshire and the Isle of Wight,* Yale University Press, 2002

Quail, S and Stedman, J, *Images of Portsmouth,* Breedon Books, 1993

Riley, R, *Portsmouth Papers No.44 – Evolution of Docks and Industrial Buildings in Portsmouth Royal Dockyard 1698 – 1914,* PCC, 1985

Sadden, J, *Portsmouth – In Defence of the Realm,* Phillimore, 2001

Stapleton, B and Thomas, J, *The Portsmouth Region,* Alan Sutton, 1989

Temple Patterson, A, *Portsmouth Papers No.3 – Palmerston's Folly – The Portsdown and Spithead Forts,* PCC, 1985

Triggs, A, *Portsmouth – A History in Hiding,* Ensign Publications, 1989

Winton, J, *The Naval Heritage of Portsmouth,* Ensign Publications, 1994

Guides and leaflets to: Portsmouth Cathedral; St Ann's church, HM Naval Base; St Agatha's church, Landport; St George's church, Portsea; St Hubert's chapel, Idsworth; St James'-without-the-priory-gate church, Southwick; St Mary's church, Portchester; St Mary's church, Kingston; The Royal Garrison church; Portsmouth Historic Dockyard; HMS *Victory*; Portsmouth City Museum, Art Gallery and Records Office; Portsmouth Natural History Museum; Charles Dickens' Birthplace Museum; the D-Day Museum and Overlord Tapestry; Eastney Pumping Station; Explosion Museum of Naval Firepower; the Royal Armouries – Fort Nelson; the Royal Marines Museum; the Royal Navy Submarine Museum; Treadgold Industrial Heritage Museum; Southsea Castle; Spitbank Fort; the History of Hilsea Lines; the Wildlife of Hilsea Lines; Gosport Millennium Promenade Trail; Titchfield Trail; Thomas Ellis Owen – *A Walk in Owen's Southsea;* Fareham Visitors Guide; Gosport and Lee-on-the-Solent Visitors Guide; the Forest of Bere; Queen Elizabeth Country Park; The Hampshire Brewery, Horndean – George Gale & Co Ltd; Royal Hospital Haslar; D-Day 60 Commemorations; Portsmouth Football Club – *Portsmouth's Road to Glory*

Web Site information for: The Boardwalk – Port Solent; History of Gunwharf Quays; History and restoration of the King's Theatre; History of the New Theatre Royal; Pompey – club history; Spinnaker Tower; University of Portsmouth – facts and figures.